A New Twist on
Strips 'n Curves

Featuring Swirl, Half Clamshell, Free-Form Curves & Strips 'n Circles

Louisa L. Smith

 C&T PUBLISHING

Text © 2007 Louisa L. Smith

Artwork © 2007 C&T Publishing, Inc.

Publisher: Amy Marson

Editorial Director: Gailen Runge

Acquisitions Editor: Jan Grigsby

Editor: Darra Williamson

Technical Editors: Carolyn Aune and Elin Thomas

Copyeditor/Proofreader: Wordfirm, Inc.

Cover Designer: Kristen Yenche

Design Director/Book Designer: Kristy K. Zacharias

Illustrator: John Heisch

Production Coodinator: Tim Manibusan

Photography: Luke Mulks, Sharon Risedorph, and
Louisa L. Smith unless otherwise noted

Published by C&T Publishing, Inc., P.O. Box 1456,
Lafayette, CA 94549

Front cover: *Trompe L' Oeil II* by Louisa L. Smith

Library of Congress Cataloging-in-Publication Data

Smith, Louisa L.

A new twist on strips 'n curves : featuring swirl, half clamshell, free-
form curves & strips 'n circles / Louisa L. Smith.

p. cm.

Includes bibliographical references.

ISBN-13: 978-1-57120-396-0 (paper trade : alk. paper)

ISBN-10: 1-57120-396-6 (paper trade : alk. paper)

1. Quilting--Patterns. 2. Strip quilting--Patterns. I. Title.

TT835.S5638 2007

746.46'041--dc22

2006023657

Printed in China

10 9 8 7 6 5 4 3

Contents

Acknowledgments

I owe many thanks to the wonderful people who helped and supported me in the creation of this book:

- A special thank-you to my dear friend Connie Barry. You are always willing to read the first draft and encourage me to carry on.

- Thank you to all the quilters from the Bayberry Winter Retreats on Cape Cod. You were incredibly enthusiastic and willing to try something new. Without your support and creativity, this book might not have been possible.

- Thank you from the bottom of my heart to my support group, Fiber Visions of Colorado, the most talented group of artists I know! You are always there for me.

- Thank you so much to the many quilters from all over the country who were willing to try something new and who have contributed so many wonderful quilts to this book! I am blessed to have so many friends.

- And, of course, a great big thanks to my husband and my mother for all the help and for giving me the time to write and create, and to my daughter, Lisa, for collaborating on these new designs.

Let's Get Started

Here it is at last: a follow-up to my favorite quilting technique, Strips 'n Curves, and to my first book, *Strips 'n Curves: A New Spin on Strip Piecing* (C&T Publishing, 2001). The Strips 'n Curves technique involves piecing fabric strips into strip sets, or *strata,* and cutting the strata into large Drunkard's Path shapes. The curved shapes are then assembled in a variety of configurations, resulting in all kinds of creative quilt options.

It is no overstatement to say I was truly overwhelmed by the enthusiasm with which *Strips 'n Curves* was received. Many of you were as swept off your feet by creating colorful strata as I was. This wonderful response gave me the courage to write again. I have had great fun creating exciting new methods and designs for the Strips 'n Curves technique. My hope is that this new publication will inspire you even more.

I have separated this book into seven chapters. Chapter One contains more template play and gives you two new designs that use templates. Chapter Two deals with template-free designs starring strata and circles—*lots* of circles. Chapter Three introduces some new ideas for using the old favorites from the first book, with the addition of paper piecing, crosscutting, and overlapping circles. Chapter Four addresses the wonderful possibilities for embellishment presented by these dramatic quilts, and Chapter Five covers quilting them. Chapter Six presents a gallery of amazing work that I hope will inspire you—everything from quilts and other items for home decor to clothing that features the Strips 'n Curves technique. Last, but not least, in Chapter Seven, I've included step-by-step instructions for four fabulous quilts incorporating many of the new techniques you'll learn in this book. But first, an introductory word about color and strata, and some general information you'll need to get started.

Color Still Makes the Quilt

Color is one of the most important elements to consider when making a quilt. Although color is often the starting point, for many quilters it turns out to be the biggest obstacle as well. I would like to share my method of working to make selecting fabric an easier and more pleasant experience.

As I work with the various Strips 'n Curves techniques, I think of the fabrics as my paints. With the Strips 'n Curves method, I am creating my own fabric by cutting and then sewing many strips together. Ideally, the strips and the resulting strata should flow together like a wonderful painting. Having many strips in lots of colors and prints (or visual textures) to work with makes this a successful process. The idea is not to have the strata go from light to medium to dark, but to have changes in value in many places, so that waves of color appear to flow all over the surface.

Before heading to your favorite quilt shop, take a moment to view the wonderful quilts throughout this book. Make sure to read Figuring Yardage (page 14), which will help you determine how much fabric to buy.

I have heard from many fans of *Strips 'n Curves,* and from students in my classes, that they like to see photographs of both the quilts and the strata used to create them, because seeing both helps with fabric selection. Here are three quilts and their matching strata to get you started. I've also included the focus fabric, when available, and the template or technique used to create the quilt. More about templates and techniques later.

A River Runs Through It *(Half Clamshell), 52″ × 46″, by*
Joan Elizabeth Rossi, Fort Collins, CO, 2004

Strata sample and focus fabric for
A River Runs Through It

You Have to Kiss a Lot of Frogs *(Free-Form Curves),*
39˝ × 43˝, by Vicki Carlson, Fort Collins, CO, 2006

Strata sample for
You Have to Kiss a Lot of Frogs

Freestyle Fish & Strips *(Free-Form Curves),*
32$\frac{1}{2}$″ × 38″, by Carol Strong, Harvest, AL, 2006

Strata sample and focus fabric for
Freestyle Fish & Strips

The most successful way to choose colors for Strips 'n Curves quilts is really quite simple. Start with a wonderful print—one with lots of color. Don't choose a tone-on-tone print; instead choose an interesting multicolored geometric, large-scale, or otherwise exciting print. I find it most helpful to choose a fabric that contains *at least* three colors. This fabric will be your focus fabric and will guide you to your other color choices. Keep a sample of this fabric with you at all times.

Go through your stash and pick all the fabrics that even remotely color coordinate with this focus fabric. Cut small pieces of these selected fabrics and staple them to an 8½" × 11" piece of white paper. Place the fabrics in order from lightest to darkest, so you will quickly discover just where and what value is underrepresented—or lacking. Now head for your quilt shop and fill in any gaps in your selections. The photographs below are good examples of a fabric mock-up and the resulting strata. You will also find it helpful to refer to the quilts *Reflectance* (page 54) and *Tropic of Capricorn* (page

55) because they were created with the fabrics in these sample photographs.

Some designs need more light fabrics than others, and it may be difficult to find many light-colored fabrics in your stash or your quilt shops. Remember, however, that some fabrics can play a dual role: both sides can be used. A fabric of dark or medium value on the front may have a reverse side that turns out to be outstanding as a light value.

My own method of shopping is quite similar to the one I've just described, based on a focus fabric and fabric mock-up. However, I have also been taking photographs of nature and collecting photographs from magazines. Color is really what turns me on, and I find you can't do better than Mother Nature when it comes to suggesting a perfect color scheme. I choose a photograph, make a color copy, and shop with this image just as I would a piece of focus fabric. This photograph becomes my inspiration, and I buy any and all fabrics I think will coordinate with the colors in this picture.

The 8½" × 11" mock-up, the strata, and focus fabrics for **Reflectance** *(page 54) and* **Tropic of Capricorn** *(page 55)*

A New Dawn *(Half Clamshell),*
61˝ × 48˝, by Louisa L. Smith, 2005

The colors for *A New Dawn* were selected with the aid of a photograph of a favorite Monet painting, *The Artist's Garden at Giverny* (1900). For information about this painting, see Resources (page 85).

Cutting

A word about rotary cutters: through the years, I have done my fair share of cutting, and my favorite cutter is the 45mm Omnigrid (see Resources on page 85). I find the handle comfortable and easy to hold. The only downside is that this particular cutter does not come also in the smaller, 28mm size, which maneuvers so easily around curves.

I have also had wonderful results using the Ergo 2000 rotary cutter (see Resources). I have problems with tendonitis in my hands, and a friend recommended this wonderful cutter to me. It took some getting used to, but now I am sold. I have a lot less pain in my hands, and I have much better control in cutting the curves for Free-Form Curves designs. I suggest you give this cutter a try.

The 45mm Omnigrid (foreground) and Ergo 2000 rotary cutters

In addition, I have found a product called Cutting Edge strips, which makes cutting even easier (see Resources). These plastic strips can be repositioned on the underside of your ruler at the desired strip width. Gently slide the ruler toward the fabric, and the plastic strips will stop at the fabric edge, ensuring that you cut uniformly sized fabric strips quickly and more accurately.

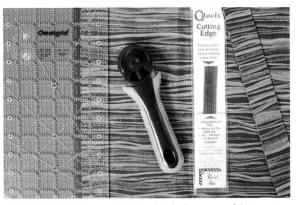

Cutting Edge strips are designed to help you cut fabric strips uniformly.

While we are on the subject of cutting, I have a special tip I'd like to share with you. I have been "stripping"—that is, working with strip-piecing techniques—for a long time and have developed a cutting technique I call Take Two: as I cut a 1½″ strip from each fabric (a size typically used for Strips 'n Curves designs), I also cut a 2″-wide strip and, if desired, a 1″-wide strip.

Why? Simply put, I find the cutting process rather time consuming and frankly a bit boring. Cutting extra strips in different sizes gives me the opportunity to make not just one but two quilts based on the same color scheme, each with a different look. I like to cut two or three strips at once and make, for example, one strata from the 1″-wide and 1½″-wide strips and another strata from the 2″-wide strips and use each strata in a different quilt. You will see some results of this method—for example, **Reflectance** (page 54) and **Tropic of Capricorn** (page 55)—in The Gallery.

When I am ready to create the second quilt, I often change the sewing order of the strips. Sometimes I add or remove a few strips. Using different focus fabrics makes these quilts appear even more different, even though they were created from virtually the same strata fabrics. I often make the quilt with the 2″-wide strips into a bargello-style—or staggered strip-pieced—quilt. I am not going to teach you how to make a bargello quilt here; many good books about this simple procedure have already been written. You'll find two of my favorites listed in Resources.

The jacket I call **Take Two** (page 64) was made using the Take Two cutting technique and strips of two sizes. The front is a Half Clamshell design with circle embellishments, and the back is a bargello design.

In *Strips 'n Curves,* the strata were based mostly on strips of the same size. In this book, I am hoping you will experiment with my Take Two cutting technique and cut strips of different sizes. Cookie Warner's quilt **Orchidaceous** is a good example of a quilt based on strips of different widths. This quilt was made using the Advanced Set of Strips 'n Curves templates (see Resources on page 85). In this case, the strata were constructed from strip sizes that alternate between the typical $1\frac{1}{2}$"-wide strips and 1"-wide strips. Cookie ultimately used a lot fewer fabrics than usual for this technique, but see how effective the result turned out to be. The fabric selection and combination of different-size strips make for an exciting quilt.

You'll find another good example of mixing different-size strips in **Memories of Marie** by Carole P. Kenney. Carole used two different strata: one with strips cut 1" wide and one with strips cut $1\frac{1}{2}$" wide. The overall composition is vibrant and exciting.

Orchidaceous *(Advanced Set),*
49˝ × 36½˝, by Cookie Warner, Fort Collins, CO, 2003

Memories of Marie *(Mixed Templates Set),*
34˝ × 38˝, by Carole P. Kenney, Providence, RI, 2005

Serenity II *(Half Clamshell),*
36˝ × 36˝, by Louisa L. Smith, 2005

The variation in my quilt *Serenity II* is another idea you may want to try. Every other strip was cut from the same fabric, and I kept the strips in the same order throughout. The resulting strata appear as a single fractured fabric. I love this method and used it again in the Free-Form Curves quilts (page 29).

You'll love this trick!

You can make your strata go a lot farther if you make sure that the color of the first strip in your strata coordinates with the color of the last strip. With right sides together, pin and then sew the first and last strip together to make a tube. This tube makes cutting shapes (e.g., the Swirl and Half Clamshell) so much easier because there are no edges to waste. I place a cutting mat on my ironing board, arrange my strata tube over it, and cut away.

Figuring Yardage

Because of the somewhat spontaneous nature of working with the Strips 'n Curves techniques, it is difficult to give you specific yardages for the projects beginning on page 68, but I can certainly make calculating your own yardages easy.

If you plan to use a fabric just for strips, $1/4$ yard will be sufficient. This amount allows you to cut a 2″- and a $1^{1}/2$″-wide strip, as well as a 1″-wide strip if you wish. If you think the fabric will be taking on a supporting role—that is, it may be used to cut whole shapes such as Circles or Half Clamshells as well as strips for the strata—then I suggest you buy at least $1/2$ yard. If you think the fabric will take on a major role—and you can have many major players in one composition—you need to buy about 1 yard. Finally, if you have already decided that a particular fabric will be used in a border too, make sure you buy at least $1^{1}/2$–2 yards, depending upon the projected size of the finished quilt.

Pressing

The seams between strips in strata are pressed open. The curved seams can be pressed either way, which is an advantage because you want to alternate the directions of the seam allowances in adjacent blocks to reduce bulk.

In *Strips 'n Curves,* I gave you a special tip for pressing the strips—namely, that you hold the sewn strips up from the ironing board at a 45° angle, so that the tip of the iron automatically pushes the seams open as you press.

A student gave me another valuable tip that I would like to share with you. I prefer to sew my strips in sets. I begin by sewing strips in pairs, and then I sew two pairs together into sets of four, and so on, opening the seams as I sew sets to each other. Although the 45°-angle trick still works, it has a tendency to press the previous seams closed. To eliminate this problem, I use a sleeve roll. This handy tool allows me to press the seams open and still be assured that the previous seams stay correctly oriented. The seams "fall down," so to speak, and are not touched by the iron. I have constructed my own sleeve roll from a wooden dowel (commonly used for constructing handrails) covered with cotton batting and muslin—voilà!

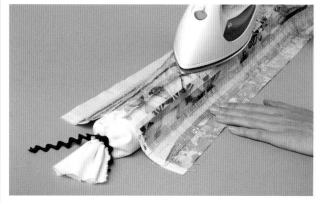

A sleeve roll is an easy solution for pressing seams open.

Small irons are also available to assist with this task. One mini iron that I have found helpful is The Quilter's Little Craft Iron (see Resources on page 85). It comes with a little stand and has a wood base to protect you and the pressing surface from the heat. One word of caution: this little iron can get *very* hot—certainly dangerous if little children are nearby—so be sure to keep it well out of reach of the little ones.

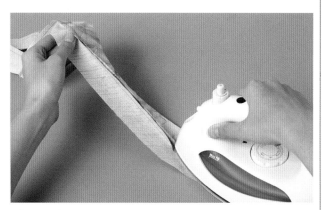

Lifting and pressing sewn strips

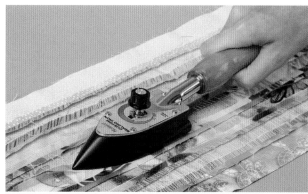

The Little Iron: perfect for pressing strata seams

Once you have cut and sewn the pieces together, it is important to press them carefully because the edges of many blocks are on the bias. Take great care in pressing so as not to press the blocks out of shape. *Press* with a gentle up-and-down motion. Do not *iron* (that is, do not drag the iron from side to side over the fabric); this will cause the edges of the blocks to stretch. I use spray starch when I press because I find that keeping the blocks somewhat stiff helps with the piecing.

The Composition

Once you have chosen fabrics and cut and pieced the necessary strata, you are ready to start composing your Strips 'n Curves design.

Check out the quilts in this book to see which look you like best and then decide which style of piecing you want to use in your own quilt. Most quilts are divided into blocks to make the construction easy. You sew a curved seam or, in most cases, many curved seams to construct a block. The ultimate goal is for the viewer to see many circles or other shapes, or both, throughout the composition—circles in colors that create depth and overlapping circles that create visual illusions—so some of these circles appear to be layered behind others. You will cut some shapes from strata and some shapes from a single fabric. You will want to place these shapes so that there is contrast where the circular shapes meet and little, if any, contrast where the blocks or straight edges meet. This placement will make the circles or other shapes emerge and the blocks disappear.

My first step is always to cut some pieces at random from the top edge of the strata, from left to right rather than from top to bottom, so that I have a good indication of what my colors (or paints) are. Then, and only then, do I start creating on my design wall. I can cut precisely what I want by placing the templates on the right area of my strata to obtain the color I want for my composition.

Sewing

When I work with circles and curves to construct a block, I firmly believe that keeping the inward-curved, or *concave*, side on top and the outward-curved, or *convex*, side underneath is the best way to go. Pinning the curve precisely, using fine pins, is also key. Sew the seam and then press it.

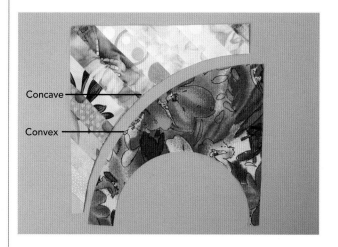

Concave
Convex

tip

I call the convex edge of the curve "the belly" and the concave edge "the cookie bite." This little memory jogger is easy to remember, and it reminds me always to keep the belly on the bottom (B&B).

These designs involve gentle curves and you can master them quickly without the need for clipping. Here's how:

1. Begin by matching and pinning the midpoints and the ends.

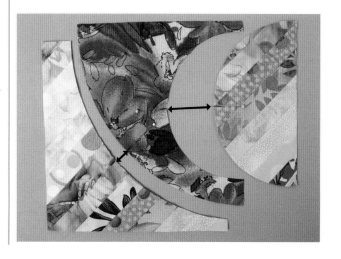

2. Pin generously with fine pins, easing as necessary.

3. Make sure the convex piece is on the bottom when you sew.

4. Press the seams.

To piece some patterns (for example, the Half Clamshell), you will need to sew a seam with two curves, so the sewing must be done in two steps.

1. Pin carefully to the center of the piece in the manner described beginning on page 15. Use a short stitch length (1.5) and sew the first curve from the midpoint to the edge of the block with the convex piece on the bottom.

2. Remove the unit from the sewing machine, turn the unit over, pin carefully as before, and sew the second curve with the convex piece on the bottom. Press the seam allowance to one side. Press the curves in the adjacent blocks in the opposite direction, always trying to eliminate bulk.

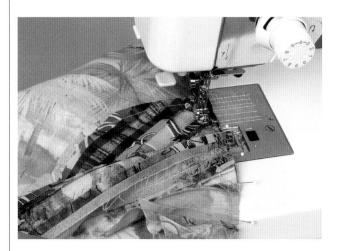

1

Two New Template Designs

The Swirl and the Half Clamshell

The Swirl

During a visit to the Rocky Mountain Quilt Museum in Golden, Colorado, I saw an antique quilt called **Orange Swirl**. I love antique quilts, and the minute I saw this beautiful two-colored quilt, I realized the shapes were quite familiar. It has the same components as the Advanced Set of templates from the original *Strips 'n Curves* book. In **Lago del Sol**, Jean Bartley used the Advanced Set to create a swirl-type design.

However, although the shapes may look similar, the Swirl is drafted in a slightly different way to create a continuation of the design from block to block.

Constructing the Swirl. Notice how the strata connect from block to block, mirror imaging from shape to shape.

Detail of **Orange Swirl**, an antique quilt owned by Pat Moore, Arvada, CO. For more information on Pat and her incredible antique quilts, see Resources on page 85.

Lago del Sol (Advanced Set),
34″ × 43″, by Jean Bartley, Billings, MT, 2005

Food Glorious Food *(The Swirl),*
61″ x 44½″, by Louisa L. Smith, 2004

To create the Swirl, start as you would for a typical Strips 'n Curves design—that is, by making
a large strata. My quilt ***Food Glorious Food*** has about 78 strips, each in a different fabric.

You can use the patterns on page 83 to make your own templates. Trace the shapes, add ¼″ seam allowances all around, and then cut out the templates. As an alternative, you can use acrylic templates that include the ¼″ seam allowances (see Resources on page 85).

Cutting and piecing the Swirl design requires some precision. Each Swirl is composed of three different shapes, but these shapes are placed in three adjacent blocks. You need to cut those three shapes—the L-Shape, Wave, and Half Circle—from the same strata piece so that the design flows from one shape into another.

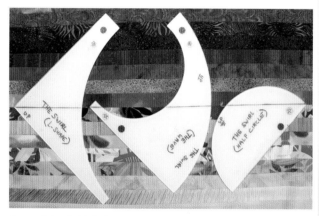

Parts of the Swirl design

It is key that you mark the templates with symbols so that you can place them easily on the correct strips of the strata to create the flow that makes this design so interesting. The design emerges when four adjacent blocks touch, as shown in the diagram below.

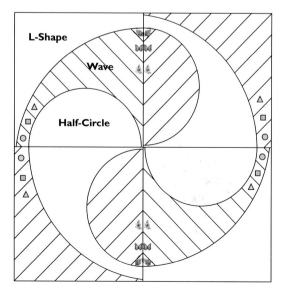

Mark the templates so the strips connect from block to block.

As you study the photograph of the Swirl on page 19 and view the various quilts made with the Swirl templates, you will notice that the mirror image of the strips is what makes the design flow. You also need to cut the shapes from fabrics with a fair degree of contrast so that the three pieces that create the Swirl are surrounded by a contrast in color. There are a number of ways you can create this contrast. One way is by cutting the pieces from different parts of the strata. For example, in one block, cut the Half Circle and the L-Shape from a dark part of the strata, and then cut the remaining piece from the light part of the strata. Reverse the positions of light and dark in the adjacent block. Or you can cut one part of the block from strata and the other from contrasting background fabric. The background fabric then plays what I call a "supporting role." If you wish, you can fussy cut and make the Swirl appear as one piece of fabric, especially where the Wave meets the Half Circle, as shown in the detail below.

Detail of **Food Glorious Food**. *Notice the fussy cutting: the Swirl appears to be one piece of fabric. For a full view of this quilt, see page 19.*

The fussy-cut fabrics in this quilt play an important role. Your eye flows from block to block, and the Swirl appears as one piece of fabric.

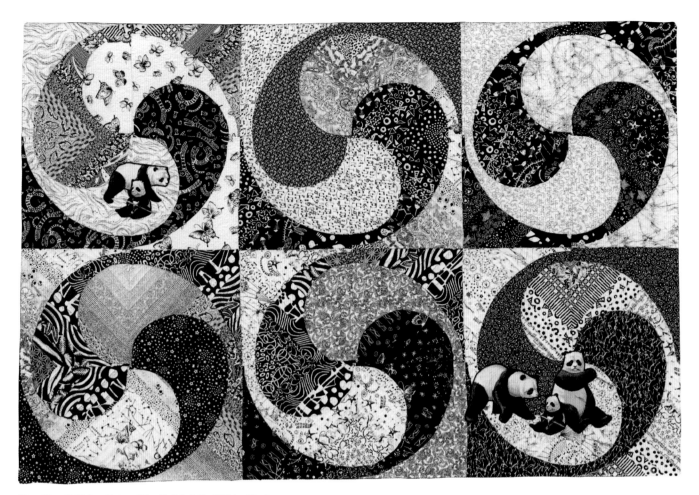

Ling-Ling & Hsing-Hsing *(The Swirl), 54˝ × 36˝, by Linda Coughlin, Franklin, MA, 2005*

If your strata is particularly light in value, then the background fabric should be medium or dark in value. The effects created by contrast are especially visible in a black-and-white version of this design, *Ling-Ling & Hsing-Hsing* by Linda Coughlin.

The good news is that you can vary the backgrounds. For example, in my quilt **Florabundance**, I alternated strata and a single fabric for the block backgrounds in all but the center block. In the center block, I used all strata to create the background areas.

Get creative and let the design develop on your design wall. The contrast between the Swirls makes this pattern come alive, as demonstrated yet again in **Renewable Energy**, a dynamic quilt by Sandy Gregg.

The strong graphic design of the Swirl is so much fun that I have no doubt you will use it to create many exciting quilts. To get you started, I've provided step-by-step instructions for **Florabundance** (page 69).

Detail of **Florabundance**. *For a full view of this quilt, see page 69.*

Renewable Energy *(The Swirl)*,
72˝ × 36˝, by Sandy Gregg, Cambridge, MA, 2004

The Half Clamshell

Now let's explore another of my favorite template-based designs: the Half Clamshell. This shape is a one-patch, which simply means that one shape is used for the entire quilt. In fact, the Half Clamshell is half of the Flowing Ribbon template used in the first Strips 'n Curves book. In the first book, we created an 8″ Flowing Ribbon template. But for the Half Clamshell, I like to use a 6″ × 12″ shape. Does it seem somewhat familiar? Well, as you may already have realized, this Half Clamshell is composed of two familiar templates, the L-Shape and the Quarter Circle of the 6″ Advanced Set (see Resources on page 85). If you place the 6″ L-Shape and the 6″ Quarter Circle side by side, you create this new Half Clamshell template. Kathy Johnson's quilt **Hooray for the Red, White and Blue** was created with the Advanced Set of templates.

Hooray for the Red, White, and Blue (Advanced Set),
53″ × 48″, by Kathy Johnson, Alexander, ND, 2004

Although the Advanced Set of templates can be used to recreate this look, you'll have a lot more seams to deal with than if you use a Half Clamshell template. Use the pattern on page 82 to make your own template or use acrylic templates that include the ¼″ seam allowances (see Resources on page 85). Refer to the diagram of this clamshell shape and note the diagonal guidelines for placement on the strata.

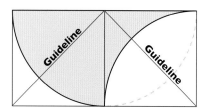

The Half Clamshell design. Notice the two diagonal guidelines.

This one-patch shape is so versatile! You can achieve incredibly interesting shapes, such as the Apple Core and the Clamshell, simply by manipulating and turning the template. Two shapes combined form my old favorite, Flowing Ribbon.

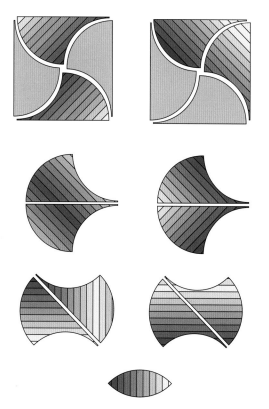

Notice the many shapes you can create with this template.

As I mentioned before, I like to use a 6″ × 12″ size because it shows a lot of the strata. For this reason, I find it beneficial to have two identical strata from which to cut. It was apparent right from the start of my experimentation with this design that if I wanted to create a certain flow in my composition, I needed enough strata to cut pieces from the same strata sections, so the extra strata came in handy. This 6″ × 12″ size also gives me the opportunity to use large amounts of focus fabric, including fabrics with very large-scale prints.

If you design a quilt using the template so that four shapes make up a 12″ block, the Half Clamshell becomes a fairly easy project—one that I would consider suitable for quilters ranging in skill from confident beginner to intermediate level. However, if you start playing with the shape and create many Apple Cores and full Clamshells, as well as the insert that I refer to as the Orange Peel, this definitely becomes an advanced technique. The trick is to play with both regular and reverse pieces. If you twist the template, you can place it so that it spills into the next half block. In other words, instead of just creating individual 12″ blocks, you can play with 1½–block units. Refer to the photograph of the shapes below and the quilt **Roman Elements** on page 25.

Either put the pieces in block formation or use 1½-block units.

Roman Elements *(Half Clamshell)*,
47″ × 48″, by Louisa L. Smith, 2003

If you place your shapes this way, identifying the original blocks becomes difficult because the individual block, as we know it, disappears. Follow the lines on the template to play with the stripes that are created by strip piecing. The design possibilities are just incredible! Be forewarned that the stitching could become quite advanced because in some cases you will need to manipulate the pieces and ease the fabric, but pinning well is a big help. You know better than anyone what your piecing abilities are. If you feel that piecing intricate curves is not a problem, than by all means experiment with the more complex possibilities this shape has to offer. I must confess that the piecing for *A New Dawn* (page 10) was quite a challenge and that I fudged a lot, but the end result of this complicated Half Clamshell piece was very rewarding!

Jungle Revelation *(Half Clamshell),*
61˝ × 33˝, by Carole Ayotte, East Sandwich, MA, 2004

The soft flow created by the curves of the Half Clamshell template makes it a favorite of many a quilter. Please take the time to flip through the pages of this book and look at all the quilts made with this design. Many have been enhanced by embellishing of some type. Carole Ayotte's quilt ***Jungle Revelation*** is a good example.

*Detail of **Jungle Revelation***

For the easiest Half Clamshells yet, take a look at my quilt *Ode to Michael* (page 60). This Half Clamshell quilt was created *without having to make a single strata!* Instead, I used a wonderful collection of fabric called Colorstripes from FreeSpirit Fabrics, designed by noted quilt artist Michael James (see Resources on page 85). The fabric is printed with 1″-wide strips and comes in a variety of colorways. If you cannot find this particular fabric, look for one with evenly spaced stripes in assorted colorways to create the look of strata.

So give the Half Clamshell a chance based on *your* piecing ability. Start off easy with the block-based Half Clamshell project *Coy Koi* (page 72) and then graduate to the more advanced compositions by playing on your design wall.

tip

When sewing the Half Clamshell pattern, I make sure the tail (the skinny part of the end) is always on the top. I insert the first pin at this tail end, and then I stretch the tail slightly to insert the second pin. From that point on, I pin as usual.

Template-Free Designs

2

Free-Form Curves and Strips 'n Circles

Free-Form Curves

The Free-Form Curves design was created purely by accident. I was playing in my studio when I accidentally made a large cut into my strata. I liked the gentle curve, and the Free-Form Curves technique was born. The result was a quilt called *Trompe L'Oeil II*.

Trompe L'Oeil II *(Free-Form Curves)*,
31˝ × 66˝, by Louisa L. Smith, 2002

I so enjoyed the freedom of this design that I started working with some students to see whether they too would enjoy the technique—and they did. You'll find the step-by-step instructions to create your own version of my quilt *Escape* on page 78. Making this quilt is an easy way to explore the process.

Rose Trellis *(Free-Form Curves),*
32˝ × 60˝, by Nancy Candelo, Davis, CA, 2005

For Free-Form Curves designs, you will need about 2 yards of focus fabric. This focus fabric should be a large-scale floral or other colorful print. Make sure the images are large enough so that when the fabric is cut and re-pieced with alternating fabric strips, the print will still be recognizable. In her quilt **Freestyle Fish & Strips** (page 8), Carol Strong used two wonderful batik panels as focus fabric.

As a rule, I prefer my large-print focus fabric to have lots of negative, or background, space. Note the black space between the flowers in **Trompe L'Oeil II**. If the focus fabric is quite bold and *does not* have a lot of negative space, it may become a problem. I have discovered that if my focus fabric is indeed becoming too strong in the composition, the best strategy is to play it up. Repetition is the answer. Our eyes like repetition, as you can clearly see in Nancy Candelo's quilt **Rose Trellis**. The flowers in her focus fabric are quite bold, but by repeating them, she unified the composition and made it work. The flowers are appliquéd all over the quilt top, thereby becoming an important part of this quilt. As I say, they "tell the rest of the story."

Besides the focus fabric, you will need about 1 yard of a secondary fabric. The focus fabric and secondary fabric need to work together. You also will need two 1½"-wide strips each from 18 different fabrics that color coordinate with your previous two choices and that gradate from dark to light. You will use these strips for the two strata required for this technique. One strata includes one set of strips in order from 1 to 18 alternated with 18 strips of your focus fabric. The second strata is constructed in the same manner as the first, but this time you substitute the secondary fabric for the focus fabric and use the remaining set of strips in reverse order from 18 to 1.

Over time I have learned that it is much easier to have a bit of contrast between the strata and the various other fabrics in this design. If the focus fabric, the secondary fabric, and the strata are all the same value, you may have a problem. In the project quilt *Escape* (page 78), I purposely worked with low-contrast fabrics, but by adding a bit of black-and-white fabric and some appliqués, I think I created a successful composition. The circular shapes make your eye travel over the whole quilt surface.

In *You Have to Kiss a Lot of Frogs* (page 7), Vicki Carlson dealt with a similar challenge, because the

focus fabric and the secondary fabric she originally chose were very similar. She decided to use a plain black fabric and not to use the second strata—in fact, that rejected strata ended up becoming my favorite vest (page 66). The solid black fabric resulted in the two silhouettes and assumed an important role in Vicki's quilt.

No templates are needed for the Free-Form Curves technique; you just cut gentle curves right across your strata or your remaining focus and secondary fabrics. It is fun and quite simple, as long as you keep the curves gentle and avoid mountains and valleys. The idea is to compose the quilt and then play with embellishing it. In my quilt *Trompe L'Oeil II* (page 29), I planned to cut out large flowers and appliqué them onto the quilt top, but I ran out of fabric and had to go to plan B—I painted some of the images onto the quilt, hoping that they would appear to be appliquéd. Nevertheless, my tip to you is to buy enough fabric to play with.

As you study the various Free-Form Curves quilts throughout this book, you will notice that the edges are rather uneven. You can appliqué them onto a border, or you may choose to keep the edges of the quilt curvy, which I consider the easiest solution.

Strips 'n Circles

This design stars strata and circles—*lots* of circles. You create blocks by cutting small strata into half-square triangles and playing with these triangles on a design wall. The triangles can be any size. If you have lots of leftovers from previous Strips 'n Curves quilts, this method is a great way to use them up and create wonderful quilts at the same time. The addition of circles completes the composition. (You can even put circles on areas of your composition that just don't seem to work very well.)

I usually make narrow strata (e.g., only six strips wide) for cutting into half-square triangles. You can cut the triangles different ways. The triangles in the following two photographs were cut with the stripes running horizontally along the long diagonal edge.

Working with the full fabric width, you will be able to cut four or five half-square triangles from each strata. Cut precisely; if you don't cut the same exact pieces each time, the strips will not line up when you piece the blocks together. Make sure the corner of your ruler hits the top of the strata and that the bottom of the strata is always on the same horizontal line on the ruler. If you are using a square ruler, you may need to put a piece of masking tape on the ruler to ensure that the sides of each triangle have the same exact measurement and that you keep the bottom of the triangle straight.

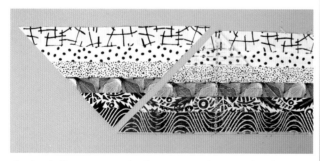

Cutting half-square triangles from strata with a triangle ruler

It is helpful to mark the bottom measurement of the desired triangle with tape when you use a square ruler for cutting.

When you cut the same two strata, it is also important to start cutting one triangle from the top edge of the strata and the second from the bottom. Let me explain. When you have a strata in front of you, the top strip may be the lightest in value and the bottom strip the darkest in value. When you cut triangles, you either have the darkest strip on the bottom or the lightest strip on the bottom.

tip

It is not unusual to get an uneven number of triangles from one strata; therefore, it is important to start cutting the second strata from the opposite edge.

Once you have cut a variety of half-square triangles, it is time to play on your design wall. (I love playing with the triangles until a pleasing composition is born!) For inspiration, take a look at the various quilts throughout the book that were created in the Strips 'n Circles format.

When you are totally satisfied with your design, you are ready to sew the triangles into blocks. Let me give you some advice: *do not* square up the blocks! If you square up the blocks, the strips will not line up with each other. Although that might not be a disaster, seeing the strips line up from block to block is quite pleasing, as you can see in my quilt *Ultimate Joy II*.

Ultimate Joy II *(Strips 'n Circles),*
49″ × 49″, by Louisa L. Smith, 2004

Keep in mind that the edges of the blocks are all on the bias. Even though you may
be used to this from working with Strips 'n Curves designs in the past, it is still worth
mentioning here. Take great care in pressing so as not to press the blocks out of shape.
If you prefer to press the seams open after sewing the two half-square triangles together,
that is fine, but be sure to *press* with a gentle up-and-down motion. (See page 14 for
more on pressing.)

Next, sew the blocks together, and put the assembled piece back on the design wall. It is time to consider whether you need or want a border (or borders) on your Strips 'n Circles quilt. Audition fabrics on your design wall, playing with the various options. You may want to incorporate some of the leftover half-square triangles into the border. You may decide you want a small inner border like the one I used in *Ultimate Joy II* (page 33).

Since the blocks have bias edges, the edges of your quilt at this stage are all on the bias as well. The edges may be a bit wavy as a result of being stretched—it's not unusual for the edges of a quilt to stretch $1^1/2''$ or more. (See Borders and Embellishment on page 45 for information about adding borders to quilts with bias edges.)

Time to add the circles. For *Ultimate Joy II*, I simply made a lot of circles—some by using just one fabric, some by sewing two fabrics together so that half the circle would be dark and half light, some by sewing leftover strata to a single piece of fabric. (This is a good time to fussy cut

circles or to add an appliqué to dress up a fairly plain circle.) For *Ultimate Joy II*, I cut my circles about $6^1/2''$ in diameter (6″ finished). I used mostly the same size circles, but you can vary the sizes. You can even overlap circles to create more depth. In other words, get creative. Try embellishment, as Sandy Gregg did in her quilt *Summer Delight*. You get the picture—anything goes, so have fun!

Summer Delight *(Strips 'n Circles),*
60″ × 40″, by Sandy Gregg, Cambridge, MA, 2004

Many wonderful tools are available for cutting perfect circles. WonderArc is one of my favorites in all its sizes (3″ to 8″; see Resources on page 85). For larger circles, there is the Cut A Round tool (see Resources). This tool cuts circles from 1″ to 12″. The inch rule for framing the circles is printed directly on the tool. Awesome! Last but not least is the CMP-3 Rotary Circle Cutter by Olfa. This tool cuts circles from $1^7/8″$ to $8^1/2″$. It is easy to use and you can change the blade when needed.

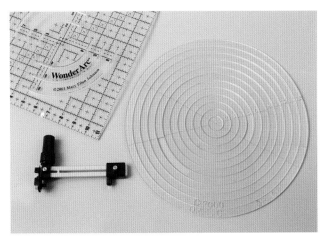

The WonderArc, Olfa Rotary Circle Cutter, and Cut A Round

Another alternative is to use freezer paper to create circles.

1. Cut a circle of the desired finished size from the freezer paper. If you are making pieced fabric circles, fold the paper circle in half to create a center crease that you can line up on the fabric seams.

2. Iron the freezer-paper circle to the wrong side of the circle fabric. Cut out the fabric circle with a generous (almost $^1/2″$) seam allowance. Set your machine for the basting stitch (or the largest stitch available). Stitch all around the fabric circle, somewhere between the paper's edge and the cut edge of the fabric.

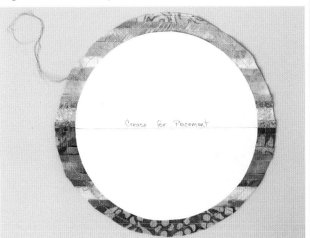

3. Leaving the paper attached to the fabric, pull up the basting stitch and then press the circle on both sides for a crisp edge and a perfect circle. Leave the paper in place for now.

4. Place double-sided masking tape on the freezer-paper side of each prepared circle and stick the circles on your quilt, auditioning various placement options. I love this method. No pins are necessary, which makes repositioning the circles much easier. I really play with the circles, auditioning them in countless positions until I think the composition is perfect. Take a look at Sandy Gregg's quilt *Many Moons*. She did a wonderful job placing the circles in her quilt!

5. When you have found the perfect placement of the circles, then—and only then—remove the freezer paper and pin the circles in place. You can either hand appliqué or machine appliqué them with a blind hem stitch. Either way is fine.

Many Moons *(Strips 'n Circles),*
42″ × 35″, by Sandy Gregg, Cambridge, MA, 2004

Give the exciting Strips 'n Circles technique a whirl with the project *Tauonic* (page 75).

3 New Ideas
for Old Favorites

In this chapter, I will share ideas for using familiar templates with a little twist. You will find ideas for the following:

- Mixing and matching using different-size templates

- Crosscutting or overlapping circles

- Combining Strips 'n Curves with paper piecing

Basic 9˝ block

Audition 6˝ Arcs on basic 9˝ block.

Use 6˝ templates to recut 9˝ block.

Pieces ready to sew

Completed new block

Mix and Match

Mixing several templates sets gives you the chance to have multiple Arcs in the Quarter Circle and the capability to put an Arc in the L-Shape. You have a better opportunity to make the colors flow, and because the smaller pieces require less fabric, you will be able to cut some Arcs from otherwise leftover strata.

Yes, mixing templates means more pieces to cut—and more piecing, of course—but it also means oh-so-many-more design possibilities! By being willing to experiment, I have learned that you can easily mix 6˝ Arcs with templates from the 9˝ sets. It is just a matter of cutting the required-size belly and bite.

Remember that *bite* refers to the concave edge and *belly* refers to the convex edge of the block. When you play with the pieces on your design wall, simply add the smaller Arcs on top of the Quarter Circles where you think they look best. Don't worry about cutting and sewing until your composition is final. (If you cut out the space, you need to fill it in.) Instead place the Arcs on top of the Quarter Circles; do not cut out the openings until you are sure. (I call this method layering.)

Refer back to Carole P. Kenney's quilt **Memories of Marie** (page 12). This quilt was constructed primarily with the Advanced Set of templates, but Carole also used the Arcs from the Basic II and 6˝ Mini Beg 'n Borrow Sets (see Resources on page 85). I think the end result is a much more interesting quilt.

Crosscutting or Overlapping Circles

If you have had success with Strips 'n Curves, this new method of playing with many sets of templates and creating incredible illusions or transparencies will truly amaze you! What you need to succeed are the Basic Set (pattern on page 84), the Basic Set II, and the 6˝ Mini Beg 'n Borrow Set (see Resources for acrylic templates that include ¼˝ seam allowances). Or use the Basic Set pattern (page 84) and draw your own patterns for the Basic Set II and the 6˝ Mini Beg 'n Borrow Set using the diagrams below. The effects possible with this simple technique continue to both excite and amaze me.

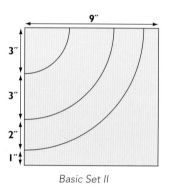

Basic Set II

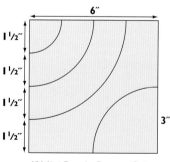

6˝ Mini Beg 'n Borrow Set

Changing Gears *(Crosscutting and Paper Piecing),*
50″ × 41½″, by Louisa L. Smith, 2005

Two of my students, Melody Randol and Cookie Warner, came up with this method.
The three of us collaborated to make a huge strata, and then we each created our own
quilt. In my quilt, *Changing Gears*—appropriately named because I now was going in a
different direction—I used paper piecing (page 43) as well as crosscutting. Melody just
used crosscutting in her quilt, but she used it a lot. Cookie opted to fuse some of her Arcs
and embellishments rather than piecing them into her quilt **Frankincense and Myrrh**.
Both Melody's and Cookie's quilts appear on page 40.

It Cuts Both Ways *(Crosscutting),*
50" × 50", by Melody Randol,
Loveland, CO, 2005

Frankincense and Myrrh *(Crosscutting*
and Fused Arcs), 43˝ × 43˝, by Cookie
Warner, Fort Collins, CO, 2005

Crosscutting creates incredible designs that suggest depth and motion, and yet the process is so simple. It takes only two steps! The key to remember is that you are trying to create the illusion of circles that move in two directions. Take a moment to review the various quilts throughout the book that demonstrate this procedure.

Begin on your design wall by placing the L-Shapes, Quarter Circles, and Arcs as usual. To create interlocking or overlapping circles, add Arcs that appear to be going in different directions from those in the underlying blocks. The trick is to lay these extra Arcs on top of the blocks—*layering is the key*. You can add layers until you have created many overlapping or interlocking circles.

L-Shape and Quarter Circle

I. Cut and piece the L-Shape and the Quarter Circle from the Basic Set as usual to create the block.

Arc cut from Basic Set II

2. To create a curve that moves in a different direction, overlay the block with the section you wish to insert. (In this case, I used an Arc from Basic Set II and placed it on the sewn L-Shape and Quarter Circle.)

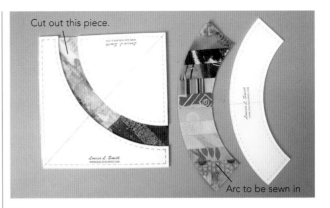

Cut out this piece.

Arc to be sewn in

3. Recut, or crosscut, the sewn block using the desired templates.

Original Arc

4. Remove and discard the old Arc. Insert the new Arc and sew the block back together again. The block is now complete. Notice the Arc going in a different direction.

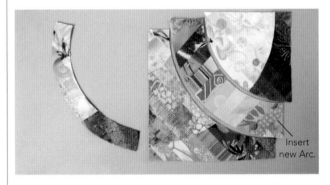

Insert new Arc.

Garden of the Groves *(Crosscutting)*,
43˝ × 43˝, by Judy Sabourin,
Medfield, MA, 2005

I cannot stress enough that these results are incredibly simple to create. Look for a moment at another quilt created using this technique: ***Garden of the Groves*** by Judy Sabourin is a stunning example of crosscutting.

Strips 'n Curves With Paper Piecing

Many interesting quilts can be created using the familiar templates, but the addition of paper piecing can make these designs even more complex and dynamic. Just trace the desired templates (including seam allowances) onto paper and cut the shapes out to use as paper foundations.

You can then use these paper shapes to create a multitude of designs by drafting or by simply crazy piecing them. The latter method is more free-form, and the points don't match at all. Piece the paper-pieced sections into the blocks as described in Crosscutting or Overlapping Circles (page 38) to complete your Strips 'n Curves composition.

tip

Fold your paper templates into multiple equal sections by folding them in half, then in half again, and so on to mark the key points of the paper-pieced Arcs. This process is much easier than drafting.

Fabric choices for paper-pieced additions can be as diverse as you want them to be. There are times when the simple addition of black and white is just what the doctor ordered as evidenced in my quilt *Mixtura*.

Mixtura (Paper Piecing), 45˝ × 36˝, by Louisa L. Smith, 2006

Cosmos and Marigolds *(Paper Piecing),*
24˝ × 36˝, by Terri Kirchner,
Mequon, WI, 2003

In contrast, in her quilt **Cosmos and Marigolds**, Terri Kirchner used a hundred different colorful fabrics! Here's good news: if you are not a fan of paper piecing but love the look, you can fuse these Arcs instead. In **Frankincense and Myrrh** (page 40), Cookie Warner used crosscutting and overlapping as well as pieced Arcs. The pieced Arcs were fused—and how wonderful this quilt turned out to be! You can use a fusible product such as Wonder Under, Steam-A-Seam 2, or any other iron-on adhesive to secure the pieces in place (see Resources on page 85). As a simple method for securing the fused pieces, you may opt to stitch the edges as you machine quilt.

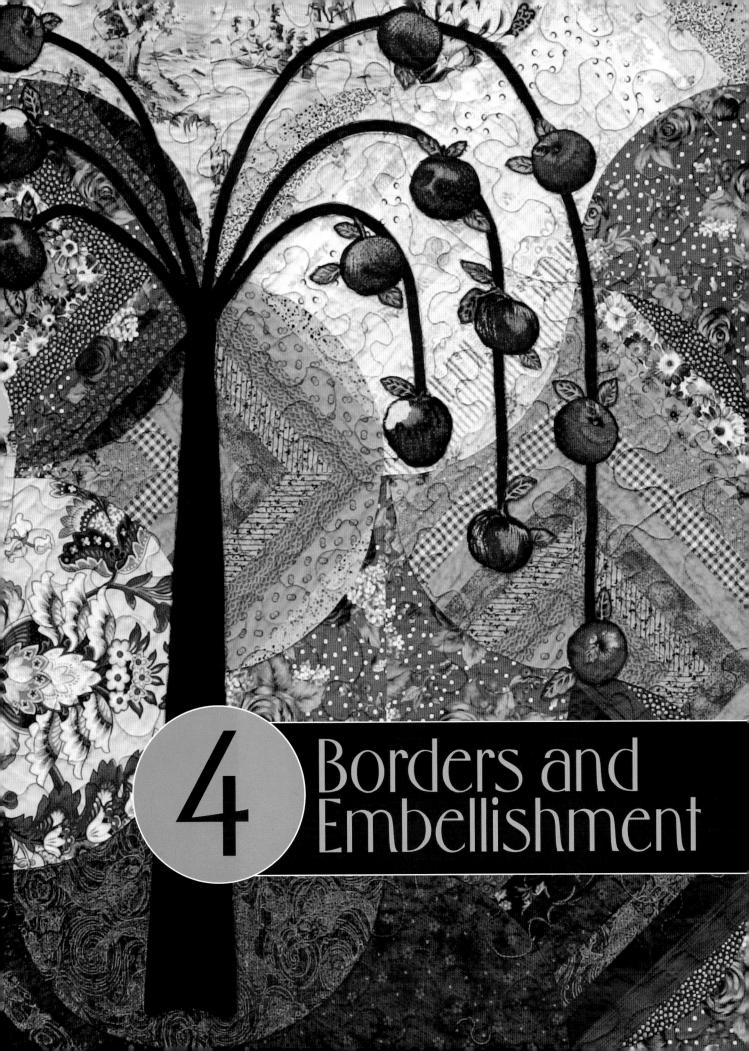

4 Borders and Embellishment

Once you have sewn all the blocks together, place the assembled piece back on the design wall. It is time to consider whether you need or want a border (or borders) on your quilt. If you decide on borders, audition fabrics on your design wall, playing with the various options. You also may decide to add a small inner border, as I did in my quilt *Ultimate Joy II* (page 33). Kathy Johnson devised a creative solution for the inner border of **Hooray for the Red, White, and Blue** (page 23) she cut up leftorver strata from the quilt blocks!

To determine the border lengths (and to resquare your quilt), measure the quilt through the center and use that measurement to determine the correct border lengths. For instance, if your quilt measures 24″ from top to bottom through the center, then 24″ is the measurement your side borders must be.

Here is a trick I've found to be helpful in preparing quilts for the addition of borders. Even if you decide that you prefer no borders at all, I recommend that you use this process before you add the quilt binding.

Select a larger-than-usual stitch length on your machine and sew about ⅛″ from the edge all around the perimeter of the quilt. Then you can simply pull up on the stitches here and there to shrink the edges of the quilt to the correct size. After you have completed this step, carefully press (don't iron!) the quilt edges.

Pull up stitches to shrink edge.

Notice the stitching used to shrink the edge of the quilt.

Once the borders are added, you are ready to embellish your quilt top. It is no secret that I love to embellish. I have always maintained that if my composition has a problem spot (or spots), I can successfully cover it up with embellishment. If I find that the completed quilt top lacks some orange, I can add orange. As I tell my students, we quiltmakers are the designers—we are in charge and can make the viewers see just what we want them to see.

In Strips 'n Circles (page 32), I talked about adding circles to the pieced quilt top. Other geometric shapes can work as well. When placed thoughtfully, these additions can make the viewer's eye wander over the composition, rather than remaining in one spot. I prefer someone to see my whole composition and not be frozen in just one part of it.

Double Fishion *(Bargello)*,
45$\frac{1}{2}$″ × 39$\frac{1}{2}$″, by Louisa L. Smith, 2004

You can also add appliqués cut from the focus fabric or other similar fabrics, as I did in my quilt **Double Fishion**. Sometimes I refer to this as "telling the rest of the story."

Red Delicious *(Half Clamshell),*
58˝ × 46˝, by Jo McCoy, Fort Collins, CO, 2004

I love the way Jo McCoy enhanced her somewhat traditional quilt **Red Delicious** with an apple tree inspired by her focus fabric. This little touch of whimsy goes a long way.

Don't be afraid to get really creative and stamp or paint images on your quilt with fabric paints. In **Trompe L'Oeil II** (page 29), I hand painted parts of the flowers because I ran out of fabric (hence the name of the quilt). Beading can add a lot of interest to these quilts. You can appliqué all sorts of images by hand or machine: traditional appliqué, three-dimensional appliqué, free-form appliqué, and so on. Wonder Under or Steam-A-Seam 2 (my personal favorite) makes it easy to adhere these embellishments to your quilt for machine stitching. Use free-motion needle painting, machine quilting, or both to securely fasten these additions to the quilt top. Notice the free-motion embroidery and quilting I used on the flowers in my quilt **Serenity II**—appliqués attached and embellished all in one easy step. Check out the flowers on **Escape** (page 78) as well.

Threads play a huge role whenever I add embellishment to my quilts. I prefer Sulky threads (see Resources on page 85) because I like the variety of colors and weights they come in. For me, it is important to match the colors to the appliqué when I satin stitch, and I also like the added bonus of the shine these threads create. On **Tropic of Capricorn**, I embellished the flowers by adding free-motion machine embroidery with black thread prior to quilting to give the blossoms more impact.

Detail of **Tropic of Capricorn**. *Notice the black stitching. For a full view of this quilt, see page 55.*

We have only touched on some of the many ways you can enhance your Strips 'n Curves quilts with embellishment. I'll bet you can imagine many more.

Detail of **Serenity II**. *For a full view of this quilt, see page 13.*

The Final Step

5

So the quilt top is done, and the last step needs to be addressed: the quilting. I suggest that you look closely at all the quilts throughout the book to see how they are quilted. In general, quilting these quilts is not a complicated process. I learned long ago that the strips are what make the quilts interesting. They do not need a lot more detail added by quilting—just a bit of emphasis through texture. But first, make sure any wobbly edges are addressed before the quilt is layered and basted (see page 46 for my trusty shrinking technique).

I have found that the quilting tends to be a huge obstacle for many quilters. I have actually heard quilters say "there is nothing wrong with just making quilt tops" because they just don't want to tackle the quilting part. Why? I've discovered that what usually creates the problem is not that they don't know *how* to quilt but rather that they don't know *what* to quilt. An easy solution is still my old favorite method: quilting through the center of the strips using decorative stitches. I use a walking foot or an even-feed attachment to accomplish this.

In Joan Elizabeth Rossi's quilt *A River Runs Through It* and my quilt *Ode to Michael*, you can clearly see how simple and effective this approach can be.

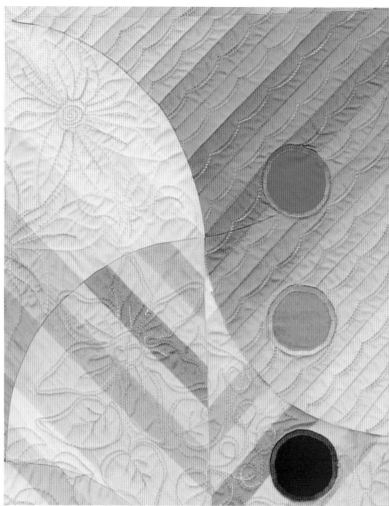

Detail of **Ode to Michael**. *Notice the stitching in the stripes coupled with free-motion quilting. For a full view of this quilt, see page 60.*

Detail of **A River Runs Through It**, *in which Joan used a variety of stitches to emphasize the strips. For a full view of this quilt, see page 6.*

You can free-motion quilt around the fabric motifs or simply meander in the background or focus fabric. This easy solution has helped many quilters actually finish a project and move on to the next one.

My Janome Professional Memory Craft 6600 sewing machine has an incredible variety of stitches available for quilting, and it has the added bonus of a large, 9″ opening, which is useful for quilting larger quilts. I must say I love this feature, as well as the fact that the machine has three sewing speeds. Many a beginning machine quilter will find this a useful feature. However, even the simplest of machines will have some basic stitches you can use. Get familiar with your machine and be patient with yourself. Learning to machine quilt is a lot like learning to hand quilt: it just takes a little practice.

I get asked quite often which thread I prefer for quilting. As with machine appliqué and embroidery, I prefer Sulky threads. I love them because they are available in such a variety of colors, and I use many, many colors in one quilt. Very seldom will I quilt an entire quilt with just one color of thread. I make sure that my thread blends with what I am quilting, even if that means I have to use nine different spools for that particular quilt. The new Sulky Blendables come in 30-weight 100% Egyptian long-staple cotton. These wonderful threads blend in with just about any fabric; hence the name. Try them—I know you will enjoy them also.

You will be amazed at how easy and fun it can be to get those Strips 'n Curves quilted and finished. Time to get busy.

6 The Gallery

Reflectance *(Basic Set),*
51½″ × 42½″, by Louisa L. Smith, 2001

This gallery is here to inspire you, to give you lots of examples of the techniques I have shared with you in this book, and to show you even more ways to use them. Let's start by exploring my Take Two cutting technique. In Cutting (page 11), I explained that you can cut strips for two quilts at a time.

Tropic of Capricorn *(Bargello),*
61½″ × 45½″, by Louisa L. Smith, 2005

Reflectance and *Tropic of Capricorn* are examples that resulted from this approach. The colors show you that they were made from the same strata fabrics, but the different strip widths, focus fabrics, and construction methods make them two totally different quilts—that is, "two for the price of one."

Strips 'n Curves Cannas *(Free-Form Curves),*
71" × 60", by Connie Carrington,
Huntsville, AL, 2005

One of the most intriguing designs ever to come out of a Strips 'n Curves class is this quilt made by Connie Carrington. Using the Free-From Curves procedure, Connie created an extremely innovative piece. Some parts of the leaves are three-dimensional!

The next two quilts are great examples of how a wonderful focus fabric can really inspire a quilt.

When Kim Solis first showed me her focus fabric for **Poppies**—a very large-scale floral print—I thought it would be difficult to use. I couldn't have been more wrong; that fabric really made the quilt! Notice how she used the fabric in her border treatment.

Poppies *(combination of the Basic and Mini Beg 'n Borrow Sets),* *45¹⁄₂″ x 63″, by Kim Solis, Ukiah, CA, 2005*

When Lisa Harris played with the composition of her quilt **Vineyard Haven**, it was the leaf print that made her quilt so exciting. Notice the leaf appliqués on the quilt top.

Vineyard Haven *(Half Clamshell),* *40″ x 35″, by Lisa Harris,* *Berthoud, CO, 2006*

Que Será, Será *(Basic Set), 116˝ × 100˝, king-size bed quilt and pillow shams, by Judy Valley, Billings, MT; Sue Hoyt, Fort Collins, CO; and Vanessa and Alvira Vechell, Minneapolis, MN, 2005*

A family in Fort Collins, Colorado, in anticipation of a family member's wedding, made her a bed quilt and then fashioned matching pillow shams, sheets, and pillowcases from the leftovers. **Que Será, Será**, the king-size quilt, was designed by one of the bride's sisters, Judy Valley of Billings, Montana, and pieced by the mother of the bride, Sue Hoyt of Fort Collins, Colorado. The pillow shams, made from the bed-quilt scraps, were designed and pieced by two other sisters, Vanessa Vechell and Alvira Vechell of Minneapolis, Minnesota. And last—but absolutely my favorite—the pillowcases and sheet set were designed by a fourth sister, Patricia Hee, of Honolulu, Hawaii. What a collaborative effort for an heirloom keepsake! It blew me away. But before all this could take place, there was a "strata party" attended by a small quilting group called Sisters in Stitches, of which Sue is a member. What a great idea to get a large strata made! There is an important lesson to be learned here: don't throw away the scraps.

Que Será, Será, *matching pillowcases and sheet set, by Patricia Hee, Honolulu, HI, 2005*

Earth and Water (*Advanced Set*),
95″ × 104″, by Barbara Cartier, Enfield, CT, 2005

Since we're talking weddings, how about **Earth and Water** made by Barbara Cartier as a gift for her son's marriage Barbara made this quilt by using the Advanced Set of templates.

Ode to Michael *(Half Clamshell),*
40˝ × 40˝, by Louisa L. Smith, 2006

What could be easier than making a Strips 'n Curves quilt without sewing a single strata? **Ode to Michael** was so much fun to create with Colorstripes from FreeSpirit Fabrics. This fabulous fabric, created by Michael James, is already printed with stripes in the perfect size.

Circles Squared *(combination of the Basic, Basic II, and Mini Beg 'n Borrow Sets), 50″ × 35″, by Carole Ayotte, East Sandwich, MA, 2004*

And then there is the quilt made by Carol Ayotte of Sandwich, Massachusetts. Carol stretched and mounted the finished quilt on double foam-core board to show off the unusual and creative shape. Her binding was stapled to the back of the foam core instead of being sewn to the back of the quilt. The result looks like a contemporary painting and is an extraordinary way to show of a piece of fabric art. I like the fact that, if you wish, you can lean it against the wall over a fireplace instead of mounting it in place. Carol's effort really inspired me—and how wonderful to know there is a way to successfully and attractively cope with irregular edges!

Strips 'n Curves designs are not confined
just to bed and wall quilts. Look at this lovely
Christmas table runner made by Shirley Mortell.

Holiday Table Runner,
25″ × 69″, by Shirley Mortell,
North Vancouver, BC, Canada, 2005

Nancy Candelo has fashioned both a quilt, **Fly Me to the Moon**, and a table runner, the latter from those all-important and ever-present scraps.

Fly Me to the Moon (Strips 'n Circles),
50″ × 57″, by Nancy Candelo, Davis, CA, 2005

Nancy's table runner, *15″ × 63″, made from scraps*

The clothing made with the various Strips 'n Curves techniques has been phenomenal as well. Let these photographs of wonderful garments inspire you.

The fabrics for my **Take Two** jacket come from a line of fabrics by David Textiles (see Resources on page 85). I cut the strips both 1½″ and 2″ wide and used the Half Clamshell design on the front panels. The back features a bargello-type design. I did not use any batting but simply lined the garment with a wonderful cotton fabric, and thus the garment is reversible. This incredibly easy pattern comes from SAF-T-POCKETS (see Resources). Since the pattern was initially designed for fleece, I made the garment one size larger than I would normally use; cotton is not as stretchy as fleece.

Take Two jacket *(front view), by Louisa L. Smith, 2006*

Take Two jacket *(back view)*

Horse jacket *(front view), by Pat Matthews, Livermore, CO, 2005*

Horse jacket *(back view)*

For a touch of Colorado, how about this jacket with the horse and matching double-sided purse by Pat Matthews?

Matching double-sided purse (one side)

Matching double-sided purse (reverse side)

Reversible vest *(front view), by Louisa L. Smith, 2005*

The little vest, which I lovingly call **Some Mistakes Are Worth It**, was made from a strata that a friend made but did not use because it did not work in her final composition. My gain—I love this little reversible vest and wear it so often that I sometimes refer to it as my uniform. See Resources on page 85 for additional information.

Reversible vest *(back view)*

Room Divider, *18˝ × 54˝ (approximate) per panel,*
by Louisa L. Smith, 2005

Now here is something completely different! I use this four-panel room divider in my guest
room. I used a different template or technique in each panel: Strips 'n Circles, the Half
Clamshell, the Swirl, and overlapping and crosscutting. All four panels were cut from one
large strata; in fact, I used over 90 strips! I think of the individual panels as mini quilts
(about 18˝ × 54˝) with pockets on top and bottom for the divider rods. I can change the
panels periodically, even inserting special panels for the holidays. How much fun is that?

Quilts to Create 7

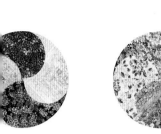

the
Swirl
PROJECT

Florabundance *(The Swirl), 54˝ × 54˝, by Louisa L. Smith, 2003*

QUILT SIZE 54˝ × 54˝   SKILL LEVEL Confident Beginner to Intermediate

Supplies

The pattern for the Swirl appears on page 83. Yardages are based on 42″-wide fabric.

▶ Approximately 7 yards *total* of as many floral print fabrics as you can find for strata. (I used 78 fabrics!) Your floral prints can be any scale, large or small; you are interested in the color more than the prints. You will need more darks and lights than mediums. Obviously I have a theme here, but you can use any theme you desire. For instance, you could use all animal prints, or all blues. Pick a theme or finally use all those fabrics you've been collecting for such a long time.

▶ ½ yard *each* of 12 to 18 floral fabrics, some with light backgrounds and some with dark backgrounds for unpieced Swirls and backgrounds. (I used strata only in some blocks and in others I made 2 of the Swirls from unpieced floral fabrics. If all blocks have 2 unpieced Swirls, you will need 18 fabrics.)

▶ 3½ yards of fabric for backing and sleeve

▶ ½ yard of fabric for binding

▶ 58″ × 58″ piece of batting

▶ Template material

▶ Permanent marking pen

Cutting

From *each* of the floral print fabrics for strata, cut:

2 strips 1½″ wide × the fabric width. (If you have fewer than 78 fabrics, you may cut more than 2 strips from some of your fabrics.)

Making the Quilt

Read The Swirl (page 18) carefully before you begin. Refer to page 15 for sewing curves and to Pressing (page 14) for pressing tips.

1. Make your strata as usual and press.

2. Enlarge the Swirl pattern (page 83) to 125% and trace each of the 3 shapes onto template plastic using a permanent marking pen. Mark the guidelines and symbols to align with the strata, add ¼″ seam allowances all around the edges, and cut out the templates. If you wish, you can use full-size, premade, commercially available acrylic templates (see Resources on page 85).

3. To make the precise design called the Swirl, you must cut 3 pieces—the L-Shape, the Wave, and the Half Circle—from the same part of the strata. Refer to the symbols on the templates and *place the templates on the right side of the strata and always on the same strip* (page 20); these templates are not reversible. You need to make 9 sets of 4 blocks each. Each swirl has 3 pieces that are placed in 3 adjacent blocks. Refer to the photograph of the quilt (page 69). You can construct each 4-block set with 2 swirls cut from strata and 2 cut just from a floral print.

4. Place the blocks on your design wall to make sure that there is a strong enough contrast in value so that the swirls are obvious—that is, so that a light strata touches a dark background fabric or a dark strata touches a light background fabric. This process will take time, and you will be rearranging the blocks quite a few times.

5. Once your composition is complete, you are ready to sew the blocks. I like to pin a block that I have removed from the design wall to a paper towel, bring it to my sewing machine, and sew. If you wish, take a 4-block set and pin each individual block to a separate paper towel, number the blocks, sew each one, and replace them after completion. This eliminates getting up and down to sew each separate block. Make nine 4-block sets.

Assembling and Finishing

1. Arrange the 4-block sets into 3 rows of 3 sets each. Sew the blocks into rows. Press. Sew the rows together and press, and your quilt top is done.

2. Layer, baste, and quilt as desired. I followed the lines on the floral fabrics and outlined some of the flowers and leaves free-motion style. I stitched the strata blocks by quilting with decorative stitches in the middle of the strips. It was easy and, I think, quite effective because the floral fabrics really make this quilt.

3. Use your favorite method to bind your quilt. Add a hanging sleeve, and use leftover strata to make a great label. You have completed your Swirl project. Congratulations!

Quilt layout diagram for **Florabundance**.

the half
Clamshell

PROJECT

Coy Koi *(Half Clamshell), 36″ × 36″, Vicki Carlson, Fort Collins, CO, 2004*

QUILT SIZE 36″ × 36″   SKILL LEVEL All levels

Supplies

The pattern for the Half Clamshell appears on page 82. Yardages are based on 42″-wide fabric.

Focus fabric and strata sample for **Coy Koi**

▶ 1½ yards of a focus fabric, preferably one with a print that you can use for fussy cutting, embellishing, or both

▶ ½ yard *each* of 3 color-coordinated supporting-role fabrics; batiks are a good choice

▶ ¼ yard *each* of 15 assorted fabrics that gradate so you have both light and dark sections of strata*

▶ 1⅜ yards of fabric for backing and sleeve

▶ ⅜ yard for binding

▶ 40″ × 40″ piece of batting

▶ Template material

▶ Permanent marking pen

*You can use strips of the focus and supporting fabrics for some of these if you wish.

Cutting

From *each* of the 15 assorted fabrics, cut:
3 strips, 1½″ wide × the fabric width (45 total)

From *each* of the 3 supporting-role fabrics, cut:
3 strips, 1½″ wide × the fabric width (9 total)

Making the Blocks

Read The Half Clamshell (page 23) carefully before you begin. You need 4 Half Clamshells to create a block. Refer to page 15 for sewing curves and to Pressing (page 14) for pressing tips.

1. Enlarge the Half Clamshell pattern (page 82) to 125% and use a permanent marking pen to trace the pattern pieces onto template plastic. Mark the guidelines to align with the strata, add ¼″ seam allowances all around the edges, and cut out the templates. If you wish, you can use full-size, premade, commercially available acrylic templates (see Resources on page 85).

2. Arrange fifteen 1½″-wide assorted strips in light-to-dark order and sew them together to make a strata. Press. Make 3 strata.

3. Sew the 3 strata into a large unit by inserting a 1½″-wide strip of supporting-role fabric in between so the strata flows from light to dark (insert dark strip) and then from dark to light again (insert a lighter strip) and

from light to dark again. The result should be a single strata that is 48 strips wide. This wide strata will give you flexibility in placing the templates and allow for cutting errors.

4. Align the lines on the template with the large strata from Step 3. Be sure to rotate the template to get the secondary designs the template creates. (Yes, you can use this template upside down!) Refer to the photograph of the quilt (page 72) and the quilt layout diagram at right for guidance.

5. Cut 24 Half Clamshell shapes from the strata, 6 Half Clamshell shapes from the focus fabric, and 6 Half Clamshell shapes from the supporting-role fabrics. If the focus fabric has a directional pattern, keep that in mind when cutting the shapes.

6. Arrange the shapes from Step 5 to create 9 blocks as shown in the block diagram (below) and the quilt layout diagram (at right). Have fun playing with the focus fabric.

Block diagram

7. Refer to Sewing (page 15). Sew 2 Half Clamshell shapes together. Keep the tail (or skinny) end on top, and the rounded (or belly) side on the bottom when pinning. Press.

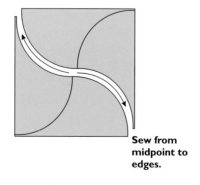

Sew from midpoint to edges.

8. Sew 2 units from Step 7 together to make a block. Press. Make 9 blocks.

Quilt layout diagram for **Coy Koi**

Assembling and Finishing

1. Arrange the blocks in 3 horizontal rows of 3 blocks each, as shown in the quilt layout diagram. Sew the blocks together into rows. Press. Sew the rows together. Press.

2. Refer to the photograph of the quilt (page 72) and Borders and Embellishment (page 45). Add appliqués or other embellishments as desired to enhance the quilt top.

3. Layer, baste, and quilt as desired.

4. Use your favorite method to bind the quilt. Add a hanging sleeve, and use leftover strata to make a great label. You have completed your Half Clamshell project. Congratulations!

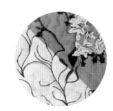

strips 'n
Circles
PROJECT

Tauonic *(Strips 'n Circles), 51˝ × 34˝, by Vicki Carlson, Fort Collins, CO, 2004*

QUILT SIZE 51˝ × 34˝   SKILL LEVEL Confident Beginner to Intermediate

Supplies

Yardages are based on 42″-wide fabric.

▶ ¼ yard *each* of 36 assorted fabrics

▶ ⅜ yard of fabric for binding

▶ 1¾ yards of fabric for backing and sleeve

▶ 55″ × 38″ piece of batting

▶ 12½″ or 15″ square ruler

▶ Masking tape

▶ Freezer paper

Cutting

From *each* of the 36 assorted fabrics, cut:

2 strips 1½″ wide × the fabric width (72 total)

Making the Blocks

Read Strips 'n Circles (page 32) carefully before you begin. Refer to Pressing (page 14) for pressing tips.

1. Arrange six 1½″-wide assorted strips and sew them together to make a strata. Make 2 each of 6 different strata (12 strata total). Make some of the strata light and some dark for contrast.

2. Place a strata face up on your cutting table. Use a large square ruler to measure for the correct triangle size and shape. Make sure the top of your ruler hits the top of the strata and the bottom edge of the strata is always on the same horizontal line. Cut a half-square triangle. Rotate the ruler 180° after cutting each triangle, so the top strip forms the tip of one triangle, and the bottom strip forms the tip of the next triangle. Cut a total of 48 half-square triangles.

3. Refer to the quilt layout diagram. Arrange the half-square triangles from Step 2 in pairs on your design wall into 4 horizontal rows of 6 blocks each—or simply play with the triangles to create a pleasing composition. This is the most important step in constructing this quilt, so take your time.

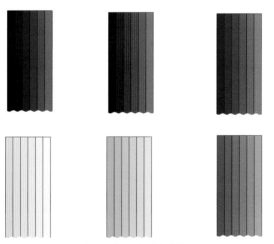

Make 2 each of 6 different strata.

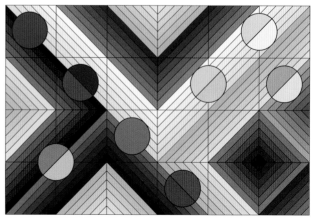

Quilt layout diagram for **Tauonic**

4. Once your composition is complete, you are ready to sew the blocks. Sew each pair of triangles together to make a block as shown. Press very carefully; the edges of the block are all on the bias. Make 24 blocks, returning each block to the layout as the block is completed. If the blocks do not appear to be the same size, *do not* square them up or they will not line up when the blocks are sewn together.

Make 24 blocks total in assorted color combinations.

Assembling and Finishing

Assembling this quilt may take a bit of effort. You hope, of course, that the lines created by the strata will line up. To accomplish this, you may need to pin at each strip, and you may also need to stretch and ease a bit. Don't worry—fabric is so forgiving. I enjoy working in this medium because I feel in control and can make the fabric do just about anything I like.

Refer to Strips 'n Circles (page 32) for guidance in adding perfect circles to your quilt.

1. Sew the blocks together into rows. Press. Carefully align the strips and sew the rows together. Press.

2. Ready to play with the circles? (This is my favorite part!) This quilt uses eight 6″ finished circles made from various fabrics, although you can use any size circles you choose. Use leftover strata, an awesome fabric (or fabrics), or any combination to make the circles. You can also overlap 2 circles. Get creative!

3. Layer, baste, and quilt as desired.

tip

If the edge of your quilt top appears to wave a bit, use my nifty shrinking technique (page 46) to make the edges as even as possible. Pin the quilt top to the batting and backing as best you can. The quilting can make your quilt lie as flat as any quilt should be. Add more quilting if you need to; for example, try more meandering where you need to work in excess fullness.

4. Use your favorite method to bind the quilt. Add a hanging sleeve, and use leftover strata to make a great label. You have completed your Strips 'n Circles project. Congratulations!

free-form
Curves
PROJECT

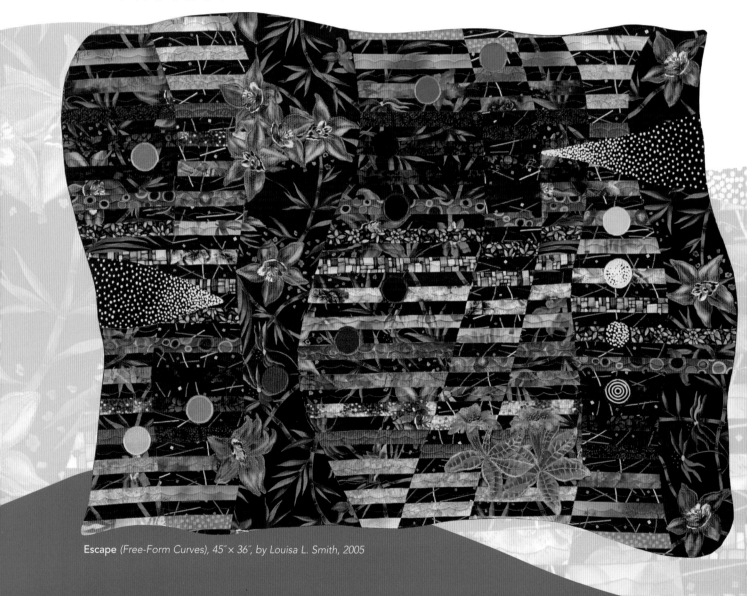

Escape *(Free-Form Curves), 45″ × 36″, by Louisa L. Smith, 2005*

QUILT SIZE **Approximately 45″ × 36″**   SKILL LEVEL **Confident Beginner to Advanced**

Supplies

Before purchasing fabric for this quilt, view the quilts in Free-Form Curves (page 29), so you understand the types of fabrics that are needed. Yardages are based on 42"-wide fabric.

Focus and secondary fabrics, strata, and additions for **Escape**

- 2 yards of large-scale print focus fabric

- 1 yard of secondary fabric; can be a geometric or small-scale print and should color coordinate with the focus fabric

- Scraps of 18 color-coordinated fabrics (two 1½"-wide × the fabric width strips *each*; 36 total)

- ¼ yard of black-and-white fabric (optional)

- Scraps of fabric for circles (optional)

- ½ yard for binding

- 1⅝ yards of fabric for backing and sleeve

- 49" × 40" piece of batting

- Permanent marking pen

- White chalk marker

- Masking tape

- Long quilter's pins

- 6" × 24" quilter's ruler

- Large cutting mat*

* A mat approximately 45" long would be ideal. As an alternative, you can tape 2 smaller boards together to get the desired length.

Cutting

From the focus fabric, cut:
18 strips, 1½" wide × the fabric width; keep them in the order in which you cut them, using a permanent marker to number them from 1 to 18 in the selvage.

From the secondary fabric, cut:
18 strips, 1½" wide × the fabric width; keep them in the order in which you cut them, using a permanent marker to number them from 1 to 18 in the selvage.

From *each* of the 18 color-coordinated fabrics, cut:
2 strips 1½" wide × the fabric width (36 total); decide how you want them arranged and use a permanent marker to number them from 1 to 18 in the selvage.

Assembling the Quilt

Read Free-Form Curves (page 29) carefully before you begin. You need 2 different strata for this quilt: Strata 1 consists of the 1½"-wide focus-fabric strips alternated with 1 each of the 1½"-wide strips of color-coordinated fabric. Strata 2 consists of the 1½"-wide secondary-fabric strips alternated with 1 each of the 1½"-wide color-coordinated fabrics, with the latter fabrics arranged in the reverse of the order used for Strata 1.

The most challenging part of constructing this design is keeping the lines straight throughout the piece. It is easy to go astray and have them tip to the right or left. Keep them vertical at all times by using pins, masking tape, or whatever it takes.

1. To make Strata 1, arrange the focus-fabric strips and 1 set of the 18 color-coordinated strips from 1 to 18, alternating them as shown in the photograph below. Sew the strips together and press. To make Strata 2, arrange the secondary-fabric strips and the remaining set of 18 color-coordinated strips from 18 to 1, alternating them as shown. Press.

Coordinating fabric

Strata 2

Strata 1

Focus fabric

2. Layer Strata 1 right side up over Strata 2, also right side up, overlapping them as shown. Make sure you have enough overlap to make the wavy cut through both strata. Pin the strata to each other and use masking tape at the edges to keep your work stable for

cutting. Use a white chalk marker and mark a gentle wavy line along the overlapped area (and I mean *gentle*—no steep peaks and valleys). The first cut is easy; use your rotary cutter to cut the wave through the overlapped area.

Strata 2

First cut

Strata 1

Marking the first cut

3. From this point on, you will cut 2 wavy lines at once. The upper one (second cut) forms the remaining edge of the previous piece, and the lower one (third cut) forms the first edge of the piece that will be adjacent to first one in the quilt. Make sure you always overlap the piece you have just cut with the adjacent fabric or strata. Overlap them just enough so you can make the 2 cuts to form a new piece, right sides facing up.

First cut

Second cut

Third cut

Making the second and third cuts

4. Every time you make another cut, you are cutting the next adjacent piece in your quilt. All succeeding cuts are done this way.

Two cut strips completed

It is important to play with the placement of these pieces. Sometimes you can have the colors in the strata's strips touch, and sometimes you can have the colors alternate. Sometimes you can use the focus or the secondary fabric, and in that case there are *no* strips to line up at all. You may need to pin the strips to each other to make sure they are lined up correctly for cutting. I like to also pin the strips on the sewing lines here and there with long, yellow-headed quilter's pins.

5. Place the cut pieces on your design wall. Take your time to play with the design. Refer to the photo of *Escape* on page 78 or look at the photos of other Free-Form Curves quilts for inspiration.

6. Once your composition is complete, sew the curved pieces together. If you are pinning strips to strips, you can pin fairly easily; when you are pinning a focus or secondary fabric piece to a stripped piece, make registration marks to be sure the pieces line up correctly. Use a white chalk marker and a quilter's ruler to make

the registration marks. The sides of the project *will not* line up; that is, the left edge and the right edge of your quilt top will have uneven edges. Do not worry about this until you have finished sewing.

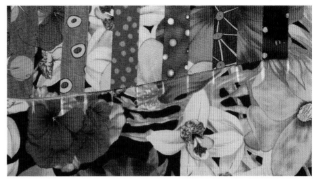

Making the registration marks

Because the edges are uneven and you can't just line the top up and sew, make sure you mark where the fabrics start and stop on the previous piece.

7. Decide whether you prefer to hang your quilt vertically or horizontally. Trim the edges of your quilt top to straighten them, or cut them curved, as I did.

Finishing

1. Refer to the photograph of the quilt (page 78) and Borders and Embellishment (page 45). Add appliqués or other embellishments as desired.

2. Layer, baste, and quilt as desired.

3. To bind the curvy edge, attach the binding and turn it all the way to the back of the quilt so no binding is visible from the front. Add a hanging sleeve, and use leftover strata to make a great label. You have completed your Free-Form Curves project. Congratulations!

Use a bias binding: it will be easier to maneuver around the curves.

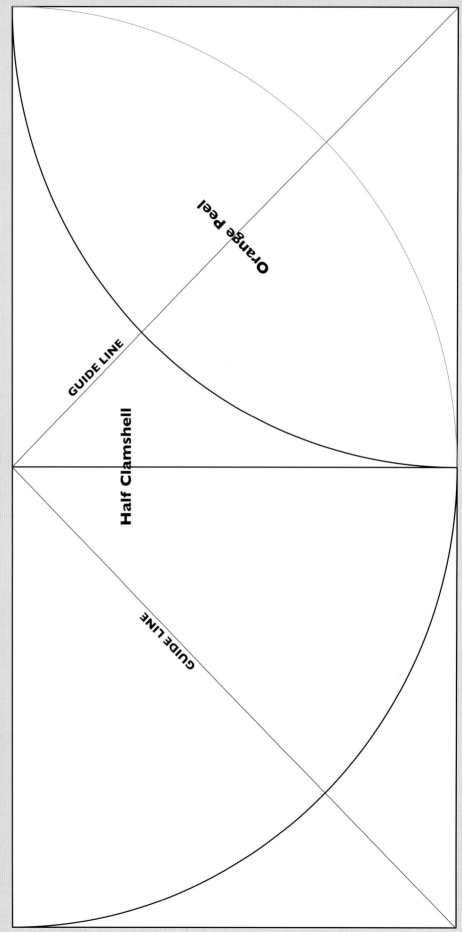

Half Clamshell Template Pattern; enlarge 125%

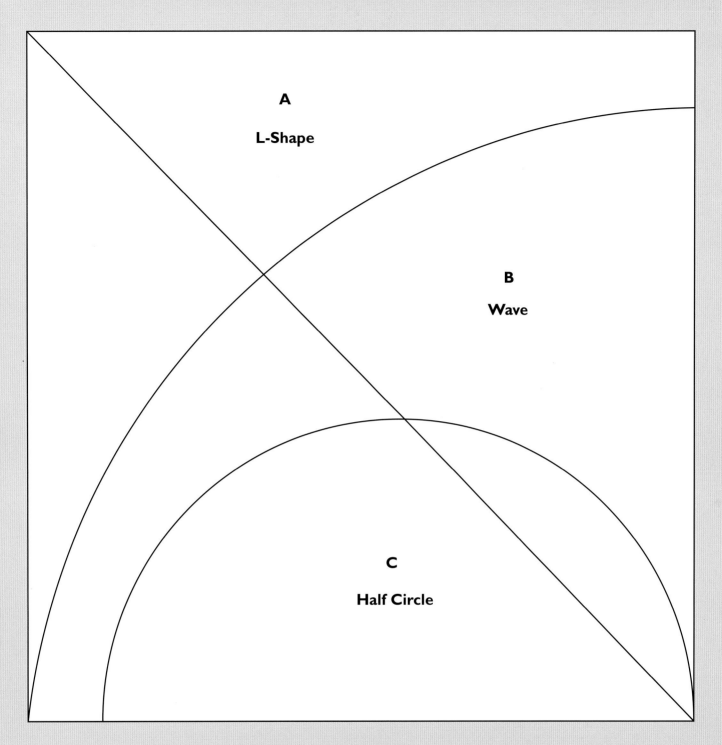

A

L-Shape

B

Wave

C

Half Circle

Swirl Template Pattern; enlarge 125%

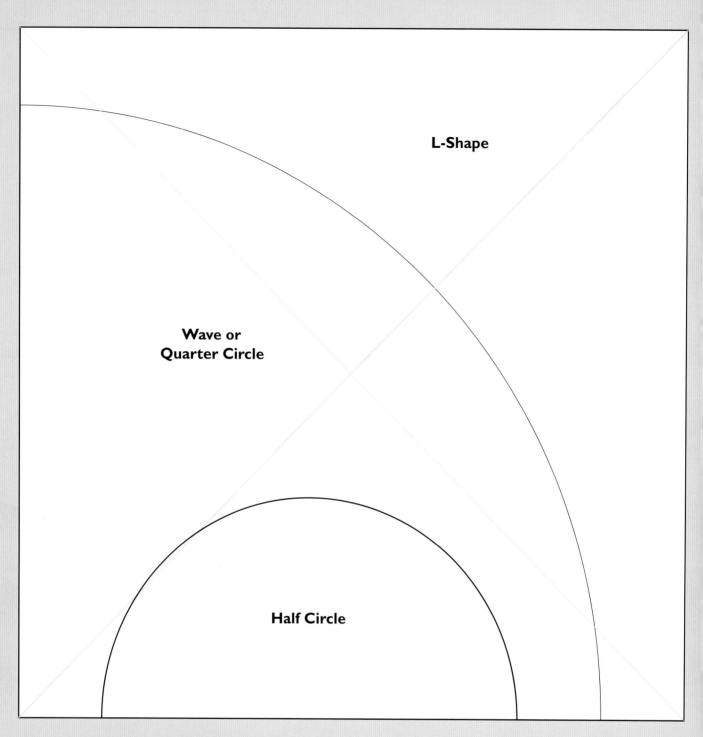

L-Shape

**Wave or
Quarter Circle**

Half Circle

8˝ Basic Set Template Pattern; enlarge 112%

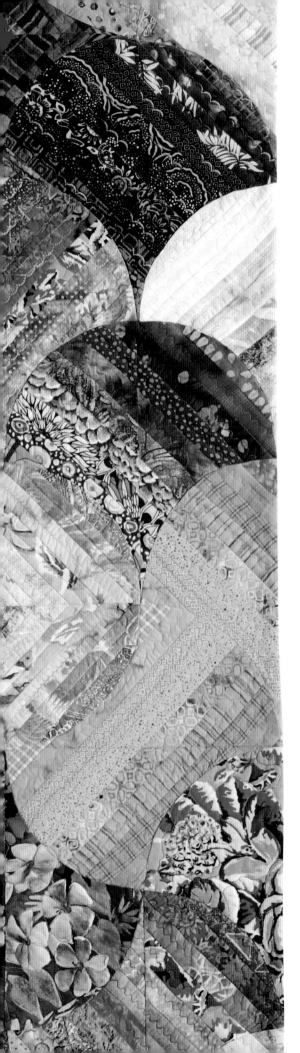

Resources

For the various Strips 'n Curves see-through acrylic templates mentioned in this book, marked with ¼" seam allowances and piecing lines for strip piecing:
Quilt Escapes, Inc.
Louisa L. Smith
4821 14th Street S.W.
Loveland, CO 80537
970-593-1265
www.quiltescapes.com

For fabric and various quilting supplies:
Cotton Patch Mail Order
3405 Hall Lane, Dept. CTB
Lafayette, CA 94549
800-835-4418
quiltusa@yahoo.com
www.quiltusa.com

Note: Fabric manufacturers discontinue fabrics regularly. Exact fabrics shown may no longer be available.

For the WonderArc Ruler:
WonderArc Designs
17300 Blueridge Road E.
Newalla, OK 74857
www.wonderarc.com

For the Cut A Round tool:
Phillips Fiber Art
P.O. Box 173
Fruita, CO 81521
800-982-8166
www.phillipsfiberart.com

For Cutting Edge strips:
Alicia's Attic
1031 Conifer #6
Fort Collins, CO 80524
888-348-6653
www.alicias-attic.com

For rotary cutters:
Omnigrid
Prym Consumer USA, Inc.
P.O. Box 5028
Spartanburg, SC 29304
800-255-7796
www.dritz.com

For the Ergo 2000 rotary cutter:
Martelli Enterprises
5450 N. West Street
Pensacola, FL 32504
850-433-1414
www.martellinotions.com

For batting:
Quilters Dream Cotton Batting
(Select Loft)
Quilters Dream Batting
589 Central Drive
Virginia Beach, VA 23454
888-268-8664
www.quiltersdreambatting.com

For the Quilter's Little Craft Iron:
Soft Expressions, Inc.
1230 N. Jefferson Street, Suite M
Anaheim, CA 92807
888-545-8616
www.softexpressions.com

For the Chaco Liner white chalk marker:
Clover Needlecraft, Inc.
13438 Alondra Boulevard
Cerritos, CA 90703
562-282-0200
www.clover-usa.com

For threads:
Look for Sulky products at your favorite sewing, quilting, fabric, or craft store, or check the Retailer Locater service at www.sulky.com.

Resources continued

If unavailable, contact:
Speed Stitch, Inc.
2298 Vale Lake Drive
York, SC 29745
866-829-7235
www.speedstitch.com

or

Uncommon Thread, Inc.
Box 11726
Rock Hill, NC 29731
www.uncommonthread.com

For Wonder Under:
Pellon Consumer Products
4720A Stone Drive
Tucker, GA 30084
770-491-8001
www.ShopPellon.com

For Steam-A-Seam 2:
The Warm Company
954 E. Union Street
Seattle, WA 98122
800-234-9276
www.warmcompany.com

For Rochelle's Reversible pattern,
#2003:
SAF-T-POCKETS Patterns
15942 SE Brooklyn Street
Portland, OR 97236
503-761-6460
www.saf-t-pockets.com

For fabrics:
FreeSpirit Fabric
1350 Broadway
New York, NY
212-279-0888 x335
www.freespiritfabric.com

David Textiles, Inc.
5959 Telegraph Road
City of Commerce, CA 90040
800-548-1818
www.davidtextiles.com

Benartex
1359 Broadway
Suite 1100
New York, NY 10018
212-840-3250
www.benartex.com

For the crazy quilt vest pattern
I used for my reversible vest:
Lunn Fabrics
317 E. Main Street
Lancaster, OH 43130
740-654-2202
www.lunnfabrics.com

For the Memory Craft 11000 and
Professional Memory Craft 6600P:
Janome-America, Inc.
10 Industrial Avenue
Mahwah, NJ 07430
800-631-0183
www.janome.com

For information on exhibiting Pat
Moore's collection of early twentieth-
century quilts:
Pat Moore
12554 W. 80th Avenue
Arvada, CO 80005
303-420-2553
Patkoerner@aol.com

For a view of Monet's painting,
The Artist's Garden at Giverny
(referenced on page 10), go to:
www.biblio.org/wm/paint/auth/
monet/last/giverny

For further reading:
Doheny, Marilyn S. *Bargello*
Tapestry Quilts. Edmonds, WA:
Doheny Publications, 1994.

Edie, Marge. *Bargello Quilts.*
Bothell, WA: That Patchwork Place,
1994.

Sandbach, Kathy. *Show Me How to*
Machine Quilt. Lafayette, CA: C&T
Publishing, 2002.

————. *Show Me How to Create*
Quilting Designs. Lafayette, CA:
C&T Publishing, 2004.

About the Author

Author photo by Fred Smith.

Louisa was born in Indonesia and educated in the Netherlands, and she came to the United States in 1960. Although her quilting started with a traditional approach, soon new and exciting designs took over, and the traditional gave way to more innovative work. The incredible flexibility that fiber offers attracted her to "paint" with fabrics. She enjoys collaborating on new designs with her daughter, Lisa, a graphic artist who shares her mother's love of quilting. Louisa resides in Loveland, Colorado, with her husband and mother.

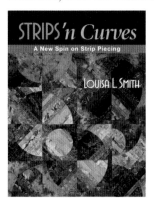

Great Titles
from C&T PUBLISHING

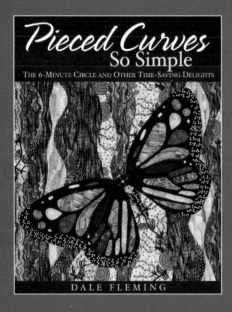

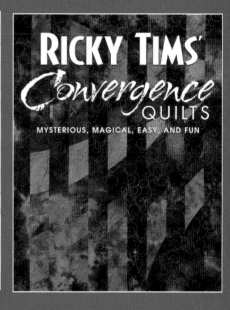
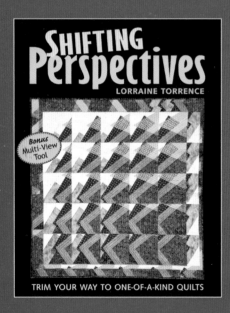

Available at your local retailer or
www.ctpub.com or 800.284.1114